THIS BOOK BELONGS TO

_____

START DATE

_____

SHE READS TRUTH

EXECUTIVE

FOUNDER/CHIEF EXECUTIVE OFFICER
Raechel Myers

CO-FOUNDER/CHIEF CONTENT OFFICER
Amanda Bible Williams

CHIEF OPERATING OFFICER
Ryan Myers

EXECUTIVE ASSISTANT
Catherine Cromer

EDITORIAL

CONTENT DIRECTOR
John Greco, MDiv

MANAGING EDITOR
Jessica Lamb

CONTENT EDITOR
Kara Gause

ASSOCIATE EDITORS
Bailey Gillespie
Ellen Taylor

CREATIVE

CREATIVE DIRECTOR
Jeremy Mitchell

LEAD DESIGNER
Kelsea Allen

DESIGNERS
Abbey Benson
Davis DeLisi

MARKETING

MARKETING DIRECTOR
Casey Campbell

MARKETING MANAGER
Katie Matuska

SOCIAL MEDIA STRATEGIST
Ansley Rushing

PARTNERSHIP SPECIALIST
Kamiren Passavanti

COMMUNITY SUPPORT SPECIALIST
Margot Williams

SHIPPING & LOGISTICS

LOGISTICS MANAGER
Lauren Gloyne

SHIPPING MANAGER
Sydney Bess

FULFILLMENT COORDINATOR
Katy McKnight

FULFILLMENT SPECIALISTS
Sam Campos
Julia Rogers

SUBSCRIPTION INQUIRIES
orders@shereadstruth.com

CONTRIBUTORS

PHOTOGRAPHER
Katie Lauritzen (Cover, 39, 47)

@SHEREADSTRUTH

Download the
She Reads Truth app,
available for iOS
and Android.

Subscribe to the
She Reads Truth podcast

SHEREADSTRUTH.COM

This book was printed offset in Nashville, Tennessee, on 70# Lynx Opaque. Cover is 100# Cougar Opaque with a soft touch lamination.

PHILIPPIANS

Philippians reminds us that in God's kingdom, things may sometimes appear upside-down.

John Greco
CONTENT DIRECTOR

Thirty of us huddled close together in the small cinder block house. It was hot, and the small "windows" in the walls left by missing blocks hardly allowed for a breeze. But our comfort didn't matter. Our host, a rail-thin octogenarian who had lived in the village her entire life, wanted to sing, and we weren't going to deny her.

I was seventeen and on a short-term mission trip to the interior of Jamaica. During those ten days, my classmates and I worked on a building project, organized a Vacation Bible School, and prayed with the sick. One of the people we prayed with was Miss Mary, a bedridden woman who just couldn't stop singing. Her memory was the only hymnal she needed, and when people came to visit, she wanted nothing more than for her new friends to join her in song.

It's been many years since I sang with Mary, but I still think of her from time to time—usually when some small thing has pushed my buttons and stolen my joy. When I remember Mary's contagious smile in those moments, I am ashamed of myself. By the world's standards, Mary was someone to be pitied—sick as a dog and just as poor. But in God's eyes, she was a princess, a daughter of the King and loved beyond measure. And she knew it.

Like Mary, the apostle Paul was a fan of singing when others might think singing is foolish. When he first brought the gospel to Philippi, he was jailed for freeing a slave girl trapped under the power of a demon—a miraculous and kind act done in the name of Jesus but one which cost the girl's masters a bit of money. Late into the night from that Philippian jail, Paul could be heard "praying and singing hymns to God" (Acts 16:25).

Years later, he wrote to the believers in Philippi from a different jail but with the same joy, saying, "Rejoice in the Lord always. I will say it again: Rejoice!" (Philippians 4:4). He had "learned the secret of being content" (v. 12).

Philippians reminds us that in God's kingdom, things may sometimes appear upside-down (see the extra on page 64). The humble inherit the earth. The last are made first, and singing is appropriate in even the most dire of situations. In this two-week Study Book, we've included several resources to help you take hold of this truth in your own life: daily reflection questions, a reader's edition of the entire letter, margin notes, theological extras like "The Christ Hymn and Other Scripture Songs" (page 34), and more.

My hope is that as you read this short letter to the Philippians over the next two weeks, you will be filled with the joy of Christ. You might even catch yourself singing.

DESIGN ON PURPOSE

You might recognize the terrazzo pattern in this book from our 2019 Galatians Study Book. For us, this pattern represents the unifying power of faith at work within the diversity of the early Church. Terrazzo is also one of the most durable types of tile, representing the enduring truth of the gospel.

By showing contrasting elements, the selected photography highlights the juxtaposition between Paul's circumstances and his joy in Christ. These include a city scene next to a greenhouse and handmade wooden doors alongside a rigidly designed staircase.

The lively aqua green symbolizes the epistle's joy and gratitude, while the dark purple is a nod to Lydia—the first convert in Philippi—who traded purple fabric.

She Reads Truth is a community of women dedicated to reading the Word of God every day.

The Bible is living and active, breathed out by God, and we confidently hold it higher than anything we can do or say. This book focuses primarily on Scripture, with bonus resources to facilitate deeper engagement with God's Word.

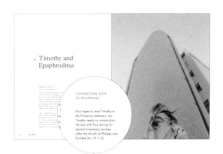

SCRIPTURE READING

Designed for a Monday start, this Study Book presents the book of Philippians in daily readings, with supplemental passages for additional context.

Throughout this reading plan, you'll find notes highlighting connections between Paul's time in Philippi described in the book of Acts and the contents of this letter, written years later.

JOURNALING SPACE

Each weekday features space for personal reflection and prayer.

GRACE DAY

Use Saturdays to pray, rest, and reflect on what you've read.

WEEKLY TRUTH

Sundays are set aside for weekly Scripture memorization.

Find the corresponding memory cards in the back of this book.

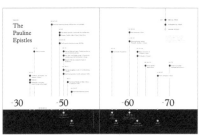

EXTRAS

This book features additional tools to help you gain a deeper understanding of the text.

Philippians   2 Weeks

PLAN OVERVIEW

The letter to the Philippians is Paul's warmest and most personal epistle. Paul wrote to the church at Philippi while he was imprisoned in Rome, thanking them for the kindness they showed him and sharing a surprising truth—despite his chains, he'd found a reason to rejoice.

Suffering can be expected in the Christian life, but because Jesus humbled Himself by becoming human and dying for our sins, we can

For added community and conversation, join us in the **Philippians** reading plan on the She Reads Truth app or on SheReadsTruth.com—where women from Los Angeles to Latvia will be reading along with you!

CONTENTS

The book of Philippians is a letter, originally intended to be read all at once. Find the insert in your book and take some time before you begin day 1 to read Philippians in one sitting.

For me, to live is Christ and to die is gain.

KEY VERSE PHILIPPIANS 1:21

ON THE TIMELINE

The traditional date for the writing of Philippians is during Paul's first Roman imprisonment from AD 60 to 62. Paul planted the church at Philippi during his second missionary journey, around AD 51, in response to his "Macedonian vision" (Ac 16:9–10). The church at Philippi was the first church in Europe (Ac 16).

A LITTLE BACKGROUND

Philippi, the ancient city of Krenides, had military significance. Renamed after Alexander the Great's father, Philip of Macedon, Philippi became the capital of the Greek Empire in 332 BC. After the Roman conquest of Greece and Julius Caesar's death in 44 BC, Philippi was declared a Roman colony. The people of Philippi were knowledgeable of their rich history and social structure, and Paul uses military and political metaphors to communicate with the Philippians in his letter.

MESSAGE & PURPOSE

GIVE THANKS FOR THE BOOK OF PHILIPPIANS

Philippians is Paul's warmest and most personal letter. After initial difficulties in the city of Philippi (Ac 16), a strong bond developed between Paul and the converts there. Paul wrote to thank the church for a gift they had recently sent him in prison and to inform them of his circumstances.

Although Paul was concerned about the divided Christian community at Philippi, his outlook was strengthened by the knowledge that Christ was being magnified. Paul's faith was the foundation of his optimism. Whether he lived or died, whether he continued his service to others or went to be in Christ's presence, whether he was appreciated or not, Paul wanted Christ to be glorified. His letter to the church at Philippi includes messages of unity (Php 1:27–2:18), freedom from legalism (Php 3:2–21), salvation (Php 2:6–8), stewardship (Php 4:10–20), and imitation of Christ's humility (Php 2:5–11).

Paul's letter to the Philippians teaches us about genuine Christian living. While nearly every theme introduced can also be found elsewhere in Scripture, it is within Paul's letter to the church at Philippi that we can really see how those themes and messages impact our lives. Philippians contributes to our understanding of Christian commitment and what it means to be Christlike.

How to Read a New Testament Letter

Most of the books that make up the New Testament are letters. These letters, also called *epistles*, come in a variety of shapes and sizes, and many are considered lengthy by ancient standards. Some were addressed to churches, while others were written to individuals. Some have been passed down to us with a name borrowed from their recipients, while others are known by their author.

HERE ARE SOME PRINCIPLES TO KEEP IN MIND AS YOU READ PHILIPPIANS AND OTHER NEW TESTAMENT LETTERS:

READING A LETTER CAN BE LIKE LISTENING TO ONE SIDE OF A CONVERSATION.

1 Because we don't always know what specific questions or situations a writer was addressing, we must look for clues in what was written to figure out what was going on.

LETTERS WERE MEANT TO BE READ ALL AT ONCE.

2 While there's nothing wrong with studying a particular passage or even a single verse, ancient letters, like the letters we write today, were meant to be read in a single sitting. Doing so allows the reader to see the author's progression of thought and make connections that might otherwise be missed.

THE NEW TESTAMENT LETTERS WERE WRITTEN TO BELIEVERS LEARNING TO LIVE IN CHRISTIAN COMMUNITY.

3 With a few exceptions (1 & 2 Timothy, Titus, Philemon, and 3 John), the letters in the New Testament were written to churches—groups of people who were learning to live as the people of God. When you see "you" in these letters, it's usually plural. These letters were typically read out loud so all could hear. They were even shared between congregations (Col 4:16).

4 INSTRUCTIONS WERE OFTEN TAILORED FOR A SPECIFIC AUDIENCE.

Not every instruction is meant to be applied by readers today. Some bits of guidance were written to counter a specific problem or abuse, while others articulate principles that are universally true.

5 NEW TESTAMENT LETTERS DRAW HEAVILY ON THE OLD TESTAMENT.

The Old Testament was the Bible of the early Church. Because it is "profitable for teaching, for rebuking, for correcting, [and] for training in righteousness" (2Tm 3:16), it was rightly applied to situations of all kinds. The better we know the Old Testament, the better equipped we will be to understand the New Testament letters.

6 THE NEW TESTAMENT LETTERS WERE ALL WRITTEN TO PEOPLE LEARNING TO FOLLOW CHRIST.

Whether they were Jewish or Gentile believers, the recipients of the New Testament letters had been rescued from the kingdom of darkness (Col 1:13). Nearly everything they thought they knew about the world and their place in it changed as a result of their entrance into God's kingdom. This new life came with its share of spiritual attacks, persecution, and mistakes. We read these letters today as fellow citizens who also have room to grow.

7 THE NEW TESTAMENT LETTERS ARE PART OF OUR FAMILY HISTORY.

These letters make up some of the earliest records we have of the Church. Much has changed in the last two thousand years, but the faith that brought hope to Christians in the Greco-Roman world is the same faith we hold on to today. Despite differences in culture, education, and language, we have much in common with the original recipients of the New Testament letters, namely the love of Jesus Christ.

8 JESUS IS THE POINT.

Though the New Testament letters were written years after Jesus's life, death, and resurrection, each and every one is about Him. These documents were penned so that readers would grow in their understanding of who He is, what He has done and has promised to do, and as a result become more like Him.

01 Paul's Opening Words

Philippians 1:1–2

GREETING

[1] Paul and Timothy, servants of Christ Jesus:

To all the saints in Christ Jesus who are in Philippi, including the overseers and deacons.

[2] Grace to you and peace from God our Father and the Lord Jesus Christ.

Acts 16:6–15

EVANGELIZATION OF EUROPE

[6] They went through the region of Phrygia and Galatia; they had been forbidden by the Holy Spirit to speak the word in Asia. [7] When they came to Mysia, they tried to go into Bithynia, but the Spirit of Jesus did not allow them. [8] Passing by

Mysia they went down to Troas. [9] During the night Paul had a vision in which a Macedonian man was standing and pleading with him, "Cross over to Macedonia and help us!" [10] After he had seen the vision, we immediately made efforts to set out for Macedonia, concluding that God had called us to preach the gospel to them.

LYDIA'S CONVERSION

[11] From Troas we put out to sea and sailed straight for Samothrace, the next day to Neapolis, [12] and from there to Philippi, a Roman colony and a leading city of the district of Macedonia. We stayed in that city for several days. [13] On the Sabbath day we went outside the city gate by the river, where we expected to find a place of prayer. We sat down and spoke to the women gathered there. [14] A God-fearing woman named Lydia, a dealer in purple cloth from the city of Thyatira, was listening. The Lord opened her heart to respond to what Paul was saying. [15] After she and her household were baptized, she urged us, "If you consider me a believer in the Lord, come and stay at my house." And she persuaded us.

1 Peter 5:1–5

ABOUT THE ELDERS

[1] I exhort the elders among you as a fellow elder and witness to the sufferings of Christ, as well as one who shares in the glory about to be revealed: [2] Shepherd God's flock among you, not overseeing out of compulsion but willingly, as God would have you; not out of greed for money but eagerly; [3] not lording it over those entrusted to you, but being examples to the flock. [4] And when the chief Shepherd appears, you will receive the unfading crown of glory. [5] In the same way, you who are younger, be subject to the elders. All of you clothe yourselves with humility toward one another, because

God resists the proud
but gives grace to the humble.

QUESTIONS

1 What did you notice about this passage? *What was your immediate reaction upon reading this passage? Did anything stand out to you?*

2 What questions do you have? *Did anything in this passage confuse you? Are there words or concepts you don't understand? What themes or questions would you like to dig into further?*

3 How will you respond? *What is the truth to be applied from this passage? How is God using this passage to teach you more about Him?*

What do the first two verses of Paul's letter tell you about his posture in writing it?

I give thanks to my God for
every remembrance of you,
always praying with joy for
all of you…

PHILIPPIANS 1:3–4

02 Thanksgiving and Prayer

Philippians 1:3–11

THANKSGIVING AND PRAYER

³ I give thanks to my God for every remembrance of you, ⁴ always praying with joy for all of you in my every prayer, ⁵ because of your partnership in the gospel from the first day until now. ⁶ I am sure of this, that he who started a good work in you will carry it on to completion until the day of Christ Jesus. ⁷ Indeed, it is right for me to think this way about all of you, because I have you in my heart, and you are all partners with me in grace, both in my imprisonment and in the defense and confirmation of the gospel. ⁸ For God is my witness, how deeply I miss all of you with the affection of Christ Jesus. ⁹ And I pray this: that your love will keep on growing in knowledge and every kind of discernment, ¹⁰ so that you may approve the things that are superior and may be pure and blameless in the day of Christ, ¹¹ filled with the fruit of righteousness that comes through Jesus Christ to the glory and praise of God.

CONNECTING ACTS
TO PHILIPPIANS

Philippians 1:3–8

Paul remembers the Philippians well, as he brought the gospel to them on his second missionary journey (Ac 16:12–40). He headed to Macedonia in response to a vision from the Lord (Ac 16:6–10) and there met Lydia in the city of Philippi. She was the first to believe, and afterwards Paul and his companions stayed in her home (Ac 16:15).

Acts 16:16–40

[16] Once, as we were on our way to prayer, a slave girl met us who had a spirit by which she predicted the future. She made a large profit for her owners by fortune-telling. [17] As she followed Paul and us she cried out, "These men, who are proclaiming to you the way of salvation, are the servants of the Most High God." [18] She did this for many days.

Paul was greatly annoyed. Turning to the spirit, he said, "I command you in the name of Jesus Christ to come out of her!" And it came out right away.

[19] When her owners realized that their hope of profit was gone, they seized Paul and Silas and dragged them into the marketplace to the authorities. [20] Bringing them before the chief magistrates, they said, "These men are seriously disturbing our city. They are Jews [21] and are promoting customs that are not legal for us as Romans to adopt or practice." [22] The crowd joined in the attack against them, and the chief magistrates stripped off their clothes and ordered them to be beaten with rods. [23] After they had severely flogged them, they threw them in jail, ordering the jailer to guard them carefully. [24] Receiving such an order, he put them into the inner prison and secured their feet in the stocks.

A MIDNIGHT DELIVERANCE

[25] About midnight Paul and Silas were praying and singing hymns to God, and the prisoners were listening to them. [26] Suddenly there was such a violent earthquake that the foundations of the jail were shaken, and immediately all the doors were opened, and everyone's chains came loose. [27] When the jailer woke up and saw the doors of the prison standing open, he drew his sword and was going to kill himself, since he thought the prisoners had escaped.

[28] But Paul called out in a loud voice, "Don't harm yourself, because we're all here!"

[29] The jailer called for lights, rushed in, and fell down trembling before Paul and Silas. [30] He escorted them out and said, "Sirs, what must I do to be saved?"

[31] They said, "Believe in the Lord Jesus, and you will be saved—you and your household." [32] And they spoke the word of the Lord to him along with everyone in his house. [33] He took them the same hour of the night and washed their wounds. Right away he and all his family were baptized. [34] He brought them into his house, set a meal before them, and rejoiced because he had come to believe in God with his entire household.

AN OFFICIAL APOLOGY

[35] When daylight came, the chief magistrates sent the police to say, "Release those men."

[36] The jailer reported these words to Paul: "The magistrates have sent orders for you to be released. So come out now and go in peace."

[37] But Paul said to them, "They beat us in public without a trial, although we are Roman citizens, and threw us in jail. And now are they going to send us away secretly? Certainly not! On the contrary, let them come themselves and escort us out."

[38] The police reported these words to the magistrates. They were afraid when they heard that Paul and Silas were Roman citizens. [39] So they came to appease them, and escorting them from prison, they urged them to leave town. [40] After leaving the jail, they came to Lydia's house, where they saw and encouraged the brothers and sisters, and departed.

Philemon 1:4–7

PHILEMON'S LOVE AND FAITH

[4] I always thank my God when I mention you in my prayers, [5] because I hear of your love for all the saints and the faith that you have in the Lord Jesus. [6] I pray that your participation in the faith may become effective through knowing every good thing that is in us for the glory of Christ. [7] For I have great joy and encouragement from your love, because the hearts of the saints have been refreshed through you, brother.

QUESTIONS

1 What did you notice about this passage?

2 What questions do you have?

3 How will you respond?

What are some ways you can practice gratitude in your everyday life?

The Pauline Epistles

AD 47–49

B Paul's first missionary journey, with Barnabas and John Mark

AD 49

B Paul attends Jerusalem Council with Titus and Barnabas

E Emperor Claudius orders all Jews to leave Rome

AD 49–52

B Paul's second missionary journey, with Silas

AD 34

B Paul's conversion

AD 50

B Paul and Silas go to Lystra; Timothy joins them on second missionary journey

B Paul, Silas, and Timothy minister in Thessalonica and plant one of the first churches in Europe

E Pyramid of the Sun construction begins in Teotihuacan

AD 50–51

B Paul spends eighteen months in Corinth planting a church

B Paul's hearing before Corinth's proconsul, Gallio

AD 33

B Crucifixion, resurrection, and ascension of Jesus*

B Pentecost

E Earthquake in Jerusalem causes damage to the temple

AD 51

B Paul leaves Timothy and Silas in Berea to continue his work

AD 52–57

B Paul's third missionary journey

AD 30

AD 50

AD 35–AD 46

P

AD 50–51
1 & 2 Thessalonians

P

AD 52
Galatians

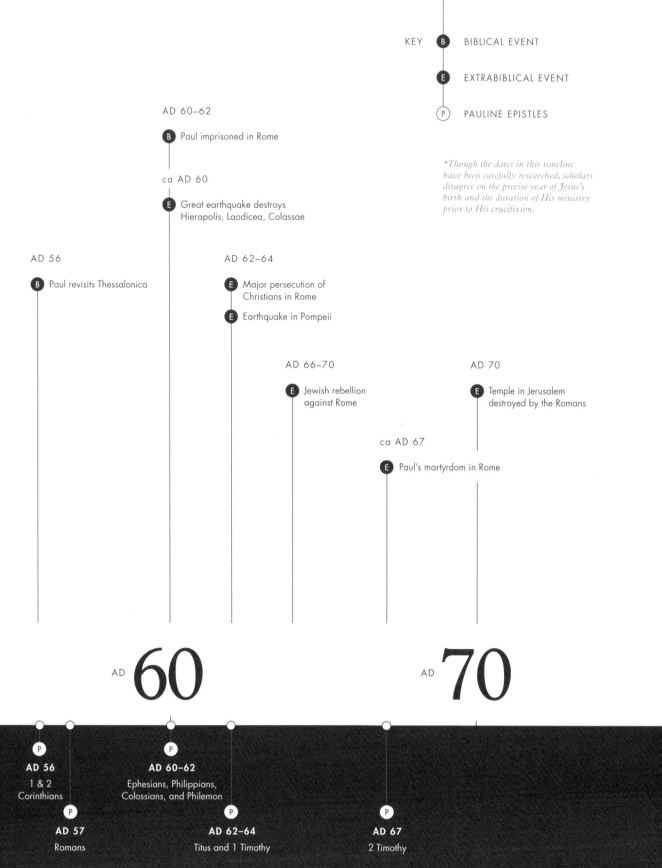

KEY
- **B** BIBLICAL EVENT
- **E** EXTRABIBLICAL EVENT
- **P** PAULINE EPISTLES

Though the dates in this timeline have been carefully researched, scholars disagree on the precise year of Jesus's birth and the duration of His ministry prior to His crucifixion.

AD 60–62
B Paul imprisoned in Rome

ca AD 60
E Great earthquake destroys Hierapolis, Laodicea, Colassae

AD 56
B Paul revisits Thessalonica

AD 62–64
E Major persecution of Christians in Rome
E Earthquake in Pompeii

AD 66–70
E Jewish rebellion against Rome

AD 70
E Temple in Jerusalem destroyed by the Romans

ca AD 67
E Paul's martyrdom in Rome

AD 60

AD 70

P
AD 56
1 & 2 Corinthians

P
AD 57
Romans

P
AD 60–62
Ephesians, Philippians, Colossians, and Philemon

P
AD 62–64
Titus and 1 Timothy

P
AD 67
2 Timothy

My eager expectation and hope is that I will
not be ashamed about anything, but that now
as always, with all courage, Christ will be highly
honored in my body, whether by life or by death.

PHILIPPIANS 1:20

03 To Live Is Christ

Philippians 1:12–26

ADVANCE OF THE GOSPEL

[12] Now I want you to know, brothers and sisters, that what has happened to me has actually advanced the gospel, [13] so that it has become known throughout the whole imperial guard, and to everyone else, that my imprisonment is because I am in Christ. [14] Most of the brothers have gained confidence in the Lord from my imprisonment and dare even more to speak the word fearlessly. [15] To be sure, some preach Christ out of envy and rivalry, but others out of good will. [16] These preach out of love, knowing that I am appointed for the defense of the gospel; [17] the others proclaim Christ out of selfish ambition, not sincerely, thinking that they will cause me trouble in my imprisonment. [18] What does it matter? Only that in every way, whether from false motives or true, Christ is proclaimed, and in this I rejoice. Yes, and I will continue to rejoice [19] because I know this will lead to my salvation through your prayers and help from the Spirit of Jesus Christ. [20] My eager expectation and hope is that I will not be ashamed about anything, but that now as always, with all courage, Christ will be highly honored in my body, whether by life or by death.

[21] For me, to live is Christ and to die is gain. [22] Now if I live on in the flesh, this means fruitful work for me; and I don't know which one I should choose. [23] I am torn between the two. I long to depart and be with Christ—which is far better—[24] but to remain in the flesh is more necessary for your sake. [25] Since I am persuaded of this, I know that I will remain and continue with all of you for your progress and joy in the faith, [26] so that, because of my coming to you again, your boasting in Christ Jesus may abound.

1 Corinthians 2:1–5

PAUL'S PROCLAMATION

[1] When I came to you, brothers and sisters, announcing the mystery of God to you, I did not come with brilliance of speech or wisdom.

[2] I decided to know nothing among you except Jesus Christ and him crucified.

[3] I came to you in weakness, in fear, and in much trembling. [4] My speech and my preaching were not with persuasive words of wisdom but with a demonstration of the Spirit's power, [5] so that your faith might not be based on human wisdom but on God's power.

James 3:13–18

THE WISDOM FROM ABOVE

[13] Who among you is wise and understanding? By his good conduct he should show that his works are done in the gentleness that comes from wisdom. [14] But if you have bitter envy and selfish ambition in your heart, don't boast and deny the truth. [15] Such wisdom does not come down from above but is earthly, unspiritual, demonic. [16] For where there is envy and selfish ambition, there is disorder and every evil practice. [17] But the wisdom from above is first pure, then peace-loving, gentle, compliant, full of mercy and good fruits, unwavering, without pretense. [18] And the fruit of righteousness is sown in peace by those who cultivate peace.

QUESTIONS

1. What did you notice about this passage?

2. What questions do you have?

3. How will you respond?

In your own words, what do verses 21–26 mean for you?

Do nothing out of selfish
ambition or conceit, but in
humility consider others as more
important than yourselves.

PHILIPPIANS 2:3

04 Christian Humility

Philippians 1:27–30

27 Just one thing: As citizens of heaven, live your life worthy of the gospel of Christ. Then, whether I come and see you or am absent, I will hear about you that you are standing firm in one spirit, in one accord, contending together for the faith of the gospel, 28 not being frightened in any way by your opponents. This is a sign of destruction for them, but of your salvation—and this is from God. 29 For it has been granted to you on Christ's behalf not only to believe in him, but also to suffer for him, 30 since you are engaged in the same struggle that you saw I had and now hear that I have.

Philippians 2:1–18

CHRISTIAN HUMILITY

1 If then there is any encouragement in Christ, if any consolation of love, if any fellowship with the Spirit, if any affection and mercy, 2 make my joy complete by thinking the same way, having the same love, united in spirit, intent on one purpose. 3 Do nothing out of selfish ambition or conceit, but in humility consider others as more important than yourselves. 4 Everyone should look out not only for his own interests, but also for the interests of others.

CONNECTING ACTS
TO PHILIPPIANS

Philippians 1:30

Paul wrote Philippians while a prisoner in Rome, but Paul was also a prisoner during his stay in Philippi. After casting a demon from a young slave girl, Paul was jailed when the girl's owners realized they could no longer profit from the dark powers that came with her spiritual bondage, and they complained to the local magistrates. The "struggle" Paul refers to is persecution for the sake of the gospel; he experienced it in Philippi years earlier and is experiencing it again in his present circumstances in Rome.

CHRIST'S HUMILITY AND EXALTATION

⁵ Adopt the same attitude as that of Christ Jesus,

⁶ who, existing in the form of God,
did not consider equality with God
as something to be exploited.
⁷ Instead he emptied himself
by assuming the form of a servant,
taking on the likeness of humanity.
And when he had come as a man,
⁸ he humbled himself by becoming obedient
to the point of death—
even to death on a cross.
⁹ For this reason God highly exalted him
and gave him the name
that is above every name,
¹⁰ so that at the name of Jesus
every knee will bow—
in heaven and on earth
and under the earth—
¹¹ and every tongue will confess
that Jesus Christ is Lord,
to the glory of God the Father.

LIGHTS IN THE WORLD

¹² Therefore, my dear friends, just as you have always obeyed, so now, not only in my presence but even more in my absence, work out your own salvation with fear and trembling. ¹³ For it is God who is working in you both to will and to work according to his good purpose. ¹⁴ Do everything without grumbling and arguing, ¹⁵ so that you may be blameless and pure, children of God who are faultless in a crooked and perverted generation, among whom you shine like stars in the world, ¹⁶ by holding firm to the word of life. Then I can boast in the day of Christ that I didn't run or labor for nothing. ¹⁷ But even if I am poured out as a drink offering on the sacrificial service of your faith, I am glad and rejoice with all of you. ¹⁸ In the same way you should also be glad and rejoice with me.

Psalm 133

LIVING IN HARMONY

A song of ascents. Of David.

¹ How good and
pleasant it is
when brothers live
together in harmony!

² It is like fine oil on the head,
running down on the beard,
running down Aaron's beard
onto his robes.
³ It is like the dew of Hermon
falling on the mountains of Zion.
For there the Lord has appointed the blessing—
life forevermore.

1 Corinthians 1:10

Now I urge you, brothers and sisters, in the name of our Lord Jesus Christ, that all of you agree in what you say, that there be no divisions among you, and that you be united with the same understanding and the same conviction.

QUESTIONS

1 What did you notice about this passage?

2 What questions do you have?

3 How will you respond?

What does it mean to "live your life worthy of the gospel of Christ" (1:27)? What role does humility play in your life?

The Christ Hymn

AND OTHER SCRIPTURE SONGS

The Bible is a very lyrical and musical book. Certain books like Psalms, Song of Songs, and Lamentations are composed entirely of poetry that can be sung. Songs also show up in other places in Scripture, such as Philippians 2:6–11, which is a passage many scholars believe was intended to be sung as a hymn.

Songs call attention to the significance of an event or a particular truth. Here are some of the key songs found in Scripture.

SONG	DESCRIPTION
Israel's Song EX 15:1–18	The song Moses sang after crossing the Red Sea on dry land. This song recounts the story of Israel's miraculous escape from Egypt and the destruction of Pharaoh's army in the Red Sea.
Miriam's Song EX 15:21	Miriam's response to Moses's song, calling the people to sing to the Lord who "has thrown the horse and its rider into the sea."
The Song of the Well in the Desert NM 21:17–18	The song Israel sang when they came to the well in the desert that the Lord had told Moses about.
The Song of Obedience DT 31:19–22, 30	A short song given to Moses by the Lord about the importance of remaining faithful to the Lord once Israel enters the promised land.
The Song of Moses DT 32:1–43	The song of blessing and warning Moses sings at the end of his life, summarizing the exodus and God's faithfulness to His people.
Deborah's Song JDG 5	A song of victory sung by Deborah, the prophetess and judge, after the Lord delivered Israel from the Canaanites.
The Song of David's Victory 1SM 18:7	The song the women of Israel sang, celebrating and elevating David's victories over King Saul's, which kindled Saul's jealousy of David.

The Song of the Bow 2SM 1:17–27	David's lament over war, in which he expresses his sorrow over the deaths of King Saul and Saul's son Jonathan.
David's Song of Thanksgiving 2SM 22:1–51	This song, also recorded in Psalm 18, celebrates the many times God delivered David from his enemies and preserved his life.
Asaph's Songs for the Temple 1CH 16:7–36; 2CH 5:13	Two songs of praise, the first sung when David commissioned the building of the temple, and the second sung when the temple was completed.
The Song of the Vineyard IS 5:1–2	A parable song, comparing the beauty of a well-kept vineyard and its keeper to Israel and the Lord.
Ezekiel's Laments EZK 19:1–14; 26:17–18; 27:1–36; 28:12–19	A series of laments in which the prophet Ezekiel mourns Israel's captivity and the coming judgment and ruin of Babylon.
Amos's Lament AM 5:2	A dirge comparing the desolation of Israel to an abandoned virgin.

SONG	DESCRIPTION
The Magnificat LK 1:46–55	Mary's song of praise and trust after the angel of the Lord told her she would give birth to the Messiah.
The Benedictus LK 1:67–79	Zechariah's song of praise at the birth of John the Baptist.
The Nunc Dimittis LK 2:29–32	The song of praise from Simeon after he held Jesus, praising the Lord for allowing him to see Israel's salvation.
The Christ Hymn PHP 2:6–11	A possible early hymn structured around the Suffering Servant in Isaiah 53, which celebrates both the humility and glory of Christ.
The Centrality of Christ COL 1:15–20	A possible early hymn expressing Christ's supremacy as Creator and Redeemer.
The Song of the Open Scroll RV 5:9–14	The song of the four living creatures, twenty-four elders, and angels in John's Revelation when the Lamb of God came to open the scroll.
The Song of the Lamb RV 15:3–4	The last song in the Bible, sung by angels celebrating the work of Christ.

05 Timothy and Epaphroditus

Philippians 2:19–30

TIMOTHY AND EPAPHRODITUS

[19] Now I hope in the Lord Jesus to send Timothy to you soon so that I too may be encouraged by news about you. [20] For I have no one else like-minded who will genuinely care about your interests; [21] all seek their own interests, not those of Jesus Christ. [22] But you know his proven character, because he has served with me in the gospel ministry like a son with a father. [23] Therefore, I hope to send him as soon as I see how things go with me. [24] I am confident in the Lord that I myself will also come soon.

[25] But I considered it necessary to send you Epaphroditus—my brother, coworker, and fellow soldier, as well as your messenger and minister to my need— [26] since he has been longing for all of you and was distressed because you heard that he was sick. [27] Indeed, he was so sick that he nearly died. However, God had mercy on him, and not only on him but also on me, so that I would not have sorrow upon sorrow. [28] For this reason, I am very

CONNECTING ACTS
TO PHILIPPIANS

○—— *Philippians 2:19*

Paul hopes to send Timothy to the Philippian believers, but Timothy needs no introduction. He was with Paul during his second missionary journey when the church at Philippi was founded (Ac 16:1–5).

eager to send him so that you may rejoice again when you see him and I may be less anxious. [29] Therefore, welcome him in the Lord with great joy and hold people like him in honor, [30] because he came close to death for the work of Christ, risking his life to make up what was lacking in your ministry to me.

Acts 19:21–22

[21] After these events, Paul resolved by the Spirit to pass through Macedonia and Achaia and go to Jerusalem. "After I've been there," he said, "It is necessary for me to see Rome as well." [22] After sending to Macedonia two of those who assisted him, Timothy and Erastus, he himself stayed in Asia for a while.

1 Corinthians 16:10

If Timothy comes, see that he has nothing to fear while with you, because he is doing the Lord's work, just as I am.

1 Thessalonians 5:12–13

EXHORTATIONS AND BLESSINGS

[12] Now we ask you, brothers and sisters, to give recognition to those who labor among you and lead you in the Lord and admonish you, [13] and to regard them very highly in love because of their work.

Be at peace among yourselves.

1   What did you notice about this passage?

2   What questions do you have?

3   How will you respond?

How does Paul describe Epaphroditus?
What would it mean to you to be
described in that way?

6 GRACE DAY

How good and pleasant it is
when brothers live together
in harmony!

PSALM 133:1

WEEK 1

WEEK 2

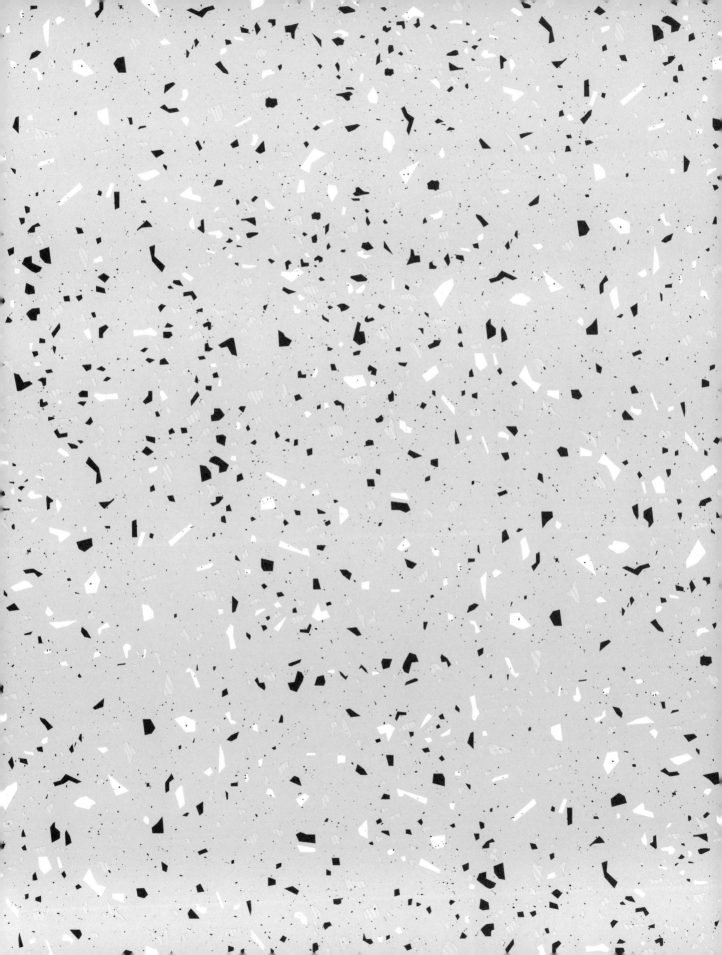

7 WEEKLY TRUTH

Scripture is God-breathed and true. When we memorize it, we carry the gospel with us wherever we go.

This week we will memorize the key verse for Philippians, Paul's declaration of complete devotion to the gospel of Jesus Christ.

Find the corresponding memory card in the back of this book.

● **WEEK 1**

○ **WEEK 2**

For me, to live is Christ and to die is gain.

PHILIPPIANS 1:21

08 Knowing Christ

Philippians 3:1–11

KNOWING CHRIST

[1] In addition, my brothers and sisters, rejoice in the Lord. To write to you again about this is no trouble for me and is a safeguard for you.

[2] Watch out for the dogs, watch out for the evil workers, watch out for those who mutilate the flesh. [3] For we are the circumcision, the ones who worship by the Spirit of God, boast in Christ Jesus, and do not put confidence in the flesh— [4] although I have reasons for confidence in the flesh. If anyone else thinks he has grounds for confidence in the flesh, I have more: [5] circumcised the eighth day; of the nation of Israel, of the tribe of Benjamin, a Hebrew born of Hebrews; regarding the law, a Pharisee; [6] regarding zeal, persecuting the church; regarding the righteousness that is in the law, blameless.

[7] But everything that was a gain to me, I have considered to be a loss because of Christ. [8] More than that, I also consider everything to be a loss in view of the surpassing value of knowing Christ Jesus my Lord. Because of him I have suffered the loss of

CONNECTING ACTS
TO PHILIPPIANS

Philippians 3:1

Paul knows what it is to rejoice in the Lord in all circumstances. While imprisoned in Philippi, he and Silas were up till midnight "praying and singing hymns to God" (Ac 16:25); see also 4:4.

all things and consider them as dung, so that I may gain Christ [9] and be found in him, not having a righteousness of my own from the law, but one that is through faith in Christ—the righteousness from God based on faith. [10] My goal is to know him and the power of his resurrection and the fellowship of his sufferings, being conformed to his death, [11] assuming that I will somehow reach the resurrection from among the dead.

Jeremiah 9:23–24

BOAST IN THE LORD

[23] "This is what the LORD says:

> The wise person should not boast in his wisdom;
> the strong should not boast in his strength;
> the wealthy should not boast in his wealth.
> [24] But the one who boasts should boast in this:
> that he understands and knows me—
> that I am the LORD, showing faithful love,
> justice, and righteousness on the earth,
> for I delight in these things.
> This is the LORD's declaration."

1 Peter 2:1–10

THE LIVING STONE AND A HOLY PEOPLE

[1] Therefore, rid yourselves of all malice, all deceit, hypocrisy, envy, and all slander. [2] Like newborn infants, desire the pure milk of the word, so that you may grow up into your salvation, [3] if you have tasted that the Lord is good. [4] As you come to him, a living stone—rejected by people but chosen and honored by God— [5] you yourselves, as living stones, a spiritual house, are being built to be a holy priesthood to offer spiritual sacrifices acceptable to God through Jesus Christ. [6] For it stands in Scripture:

> See, I lay a stone in Zion,
> a chosen and honored cornerstone,
> and the one who believes in him
> will never be put to shame.

[7] So honor will come to you who believe; but for the unbelieving,

> The stone that the builders rejected—
> this one has become the cornerstone,

[8] and

> A stone to stumble over,
> and a rock to trip over.

They stumble because they disobey the word; they were destined for this.

[9] But you are a chosen race, a royal priesthood, a holy nation, a people for his possession, so that you may proclaim the praises of the one who called you out of darkness into his marvelous light.

[10] Once you were not a people, but now you are God's people; you had not received mercy, but now you have received mercy.

QUESTIONS

1 What did you notice about this passage?

2 What questions do you have?

3 How will you respond?

What is Paul's goal in verse 10? What is your goal in the Christian life?

Forgetting what is behind and
reaching forward to what is ahead,
I pursue as my goal the prize
promised by God's heavenly call
in Christ Jesus.

PHILIPPIANS 3:13–14

09 Reaching Forward to God's Goal

Philippians 3:12–16

REACHING FORWARD TO GOD'S GOAL

[12] Not that I have already reached the goal or am already perfect, but I make every effort to take hold of it because I also have been taken hold of by Christ Jesus. [13] Brothers and sisters, I do not consider myself to have taken hold of it. But one thing I do: Forgetting what is behind and reaching forward to what is ahead, [14] I pursue as my goal the prize promised by God's heavenly call in Christ Jesus. [15] Therefore, let all of us who are mature think this way. And if you think differently about anything, God will reveal this also to you. [16] In any case, we should live up to whatever truth we have attained.

Romans 8:28–30

[28] We know that all things work together for the good of those who love God, who are called according to his purpose. [29] For those he foreknew he also predestined to be conformed to the image of his Son, so that he would be the firstborn among many brothers and sisters. [30] And those he predestined, he also called; and those he called, he also justified; and those he justified, he also glorified.

1 Corinthians 9:19–27

[19] Although I am free from all and not anyone's slave, I have made myself a slave to everyone, in order to win more people. [20] To the Jews I became like a Jew, to win Jews; to those under the law, like one under the law—though I myself am not under the law—to win those under the law. [21] To those who are without the law, like one without the law—though I am not without God's law but under the law of Christ—to win those without the law. [22] To the weak I became weak, in order to win the weak. I have become all things to all people, so that I may by every possible means save some. [23] Now I do all this because of the gospel, so that I may share in the blessings.

[24] Don't you know that the runners in a stadium all race, but only one receives the prize? Run in such a way to win the prize. [25] Now everyone who competes exercises self-control in everything. They do it to receive a perishable crown, but we an imperishable crown. [26] So I do not run like one who runs aimlessly or box like one beating the air. [27] Instead, I discipline my body and bring it under strict control, so that after preaching to others, I myself will not be disqualified.

Colossians 3:1–4

THE LIFE OF THE NEW MAN

[1] So if you have been raised with Christ, seek the things above, where Christ is, seated at the right hand of God.

[2] Set your minds on things above, not on earthly things.

[3] For you died, and your life is hidden with Christ in God. [4] When Christ, who is your life, appears, then you also will appear with him in glory.

DAY 9

1 What did you notice about this passage?

2 What questions do you have?

3 How will you respond?

Why should you continue to reach
forward to what God has promised?
What are some ways you can do that?

Give Me Jesus

In the morning when I rise,
in the morning when I rise,
in the morning when I rise
give me Jesus.

Give me Jesus,
give me Jesus.
You can have all this world,
but give me Jesus.

And when I am alone,
oh, and when I am alone,
and when I am alone
give me Jesus.

Give me Jesus,
give me Jesus.
You can have all this world,
but give me Jesus.

And when I come to die,
oh, and when I come to die,
and when I come to die
give me Jesus.

Give me Jesus,
give me Jesus.
You can have all this world,
but give me Jesus.

TEXT AND TUNE
African American Spiritual

They are focused on earthly things,
but our citizenship is in heaven.

PHILIPPIANS 3:19–20

10 Stand Firm in the Lord

Philippians 3:17–21

[17] Join in imitating me, brothers and sisters, and pay careful attention to those who live according to the example you have in us. [18] For I have often told you, and now say again with tears, that many live as enemies of the cross of Christ. [19] Their end is destruction; their god is their stomach; their glory is in their shame. They are focused on earthly things, [20] but our citizenship is in heaven, and we eagerly wait for a Savior from there, the Lord Jesus Christ. [21] He will transform the body of our humble condition into the likeness of his glorious body, by the power that enables him to subject everything to himself.

Philippians 4:1

So then, my dearly loved and longed for brothers and sisters, my joy and crown, in this manner stand firm in the Lord, dear friends.

CONNECTING ACTS
TO PHILIPPIANS

Philippians 3:20

Caesar Augustus made Philippi a Roman colony in 42 BC, and that status came with certain privileges. The people were granted Roman citizenship, were exempt from most forms of taxation, and received special land-ownership rights. In general, Philippians were proud to be Roman citizens, but Paul reminds them of what was more important: their citizenship in heaven.

Romans 16:17–20

WARNING AGAINST DIVISIVE PEOPLE

[17] Now I urge you, brothers and sisters, to watch out for those who create divisions and obstacles contrary to the teaching that you learned. Avoid them, [18] because such people do not serve our Lord Christ but their own appetites. They deceive the hearts of the unsuspecting with smooth talk and flattering words.

PAUL'S GRACIOUS CONCLUSION

[19] The report of your obedience has reached everyone. Therefore I rejoice over you, but I want you to be wise about what is good, and yet innocent about what is evil. [20] The God of peace will soon crush Satan under your feet. The grace of our Lord Jesus be with you.

2 Thessalonians 1:5–12

[5] It is clear evidence of God's righteous judgment that you will be counted worthy of God's kingdom, for which you also are suffering, [6] since it is just for God to repay with affliction those who afflict you [7] and to give relief to you who are afflicted, along with us. This will take place at the revelation of the Lord Jesus from heaven with his powerful angels, [8] when he takes vengeance with flaming fire on those who don't know God and on those who don't obey the gospel of our Lord Jesus. [9] They will pay the penalty of eternal destruction from the Lord's presence and from his glorious strength [10] on that day when he comes to be glorified by his saints and to be marveled at by all those who have believed, because our testimony among you was believed. [11] In view of this, we always pray for you that our God will make you worthy of his calling, and by his power fulfill your every desire to do good and your work produced by faith, [12] so that the name of our Lord Jesus will be glorified by you, and you by him, according to the grace of our God and the Lord Jesus Christ.

Titus 2:11–14

[11] For the grace of God has appeared, bringing salvation for all people, [12] instructing us to deny godlessness and worldly lusts and to live in a sensible, righteous, and godly way in the present age, [13] while we wait for the blessed hope, the appearing of the glory of our great God and Savior, Jesus Christ. [14] He gave himself for us to redeem us from all lawlessness and to cleanse for himself a people for his own possession, eager to do good works.

QUESTIONS

1. What did you notice about this passage?

2. What questions do you have?

3. How will you respond?

What does it mean to know that your citizenship is in heaven?

Rejoice in the Lord always.
I will say it again: Rejoice!

PHILIPPIANS 4:4

11 Practical Counsel

Philippians 4:2–9

PRACTICAL COUNSEL

² I urge Euodia and I urge Syntyche to agree in the Lord. ³ Yes, I also ask you, true partner, to help these women who have contended for the gospel at my side, along with Clement and the rest of my coworkers whose names are in the book of life. ⁴ Rejoice in the Lord always. I will say it again: Rejoice! ⁵ Let your graciousness be known to everyone. The Lord is near. ⁶ Don't worry about anything, but in everything, through prayer and petition with thanksgiving, present your requests to God. ⁷ And the peace of God, which surpasses all understanding, will guard your hearts and minds in Christ Jesus.

⁸ Finally brothers and sisters, whatever is true, whatever is honorable, whatever is just, whatever is pure, whatever is lovely, whatever is commendable—if there is any moral excellence and if there is anything praiseworthy—dwell on these things. ⁹ Do what you have learned and received and heard from me, and seen in me, and the God of peace will be with you.

CONNECTING ACTS
TO PHILIPPIANS

Philippians 4:2–3

Though they were now quarreling, Paul remembers Euodia and Syntyche as women who "contended for the gospel" alongside of him. Women played an important role in the earliest days of the church at Philippi (Ac 16:11–15). It is possible that these two women were part of Lydia's prayer group and were among the city's first believers.

Matthew 6:25–34

25 "Therefore I tell you: Don't worry about your life, what you will eat or what you will drink; or about your body, what you will wear. Isn't life more than food and the body more than clothing? 26 Consider the birds of the sky: They don't sow or reap or gather into barns, yet your heavenly Father feeds them. Aren't you worth more than they? 27 Can any of you add one moment to his life span by worrying? 28 And why do you worry about clothes? Observe how the wildflowers of the field grow: They don't labor or spin thread. 29 Yet I tell you that not even Solomon in all his splendor was adorned like one of these. 30 If that's how God clothes the grass of the field, which is here today and thrown into the furnace tomorrow, won't he do much more for you—you of little faith? 31 So don't worry, saying, 'What will we eat?' or 'What will we drink?' or 'What will we wear?' 32 For the Gentiles eagerly seek all these things, and your heavenly Father knows that you need them. 33 But seek first the kingdom of God and his righteousness, and all these things will be provided for you. 34 Therefore don't worry about tomorrow, because tomorrow will worry about itself. Each day has enough trouble of its own."

John 15:7–11

7 "If you remain in me and my words remain in you, ask whatever you want and it will be done for you. 8 My Father is glorified by this: that you produce much fruit and prove to be my disciples.

CHRISTLIKE LOVE

9 "As the Father has loved me, I have also loved you. Remain in my love. 10 If you keep my commands you will remain in my love, just as I have kept my Father's commands and remain in his love.

11 "I have told you these things so that my joy may be in you and your joy may be complete."

Romans 8:5–6

5 For those who live according to the flesh have their minds set on the things of the flesh, but those who live according to the Spirit have their minds set on the things of the Spirit. 6 Now the mind-set of the flesh is death, but the mind-set of the Spirit is life and peace.

DAY **11**

1 What did you notice about this passage?

2 What questions do you have?

3 How will you respond?

What would it look like to rejoice in the Lord always?

THE UPSIDE-DOWN KINGDOM

The ways of Jesus are not like the ways of the world. In His teachings, Jesus often flipped well-known concepts on their heads to illustrate what life in the Spirit looks like. In Christ's kingdom, suffering leads to glory, weakness to strength, and letting go of the world means inheriting the earth. In his letter to the Philippians, Paul expressed the ultimate gospel paradox: "to live is Christ, and to die is gain" (Php 1:21).

The following New Testament passages describe other realities of the "upside-down" kingdom Jesus established during His ministry on earth.

"Blessed are the poor in spirit, for the kingdom of heaven is theirs."

MT 5:3

"Blessed are those who mourn, for they will be comforted."

MT 5:4

"Blessed are those who hunger and thirst for righteousness, for they will be filled."

MT 5:6

"Blessed are those who are persecuted because of righteousness, for the kingdom of heaven is theirs."

MT 5:10

"But I tell you, don't resist an evildoer. On the contrary, if anyone slaps you on your right cheek, turn the other to him also."

MT 5:39

"You have heard that it was said, Love your neighbor and hate your enemy. But I tell you, love your enemies and pray for those who persecute you."

MT 5:43–44

"Anyone who finds his life will lose it, and anyone who loses his life because of me will find it."

MT 10:39

"So the last will be first, and the first last."

MT 20:16

"Whoever wants to become great among you must be your servant, and whoever wants to be first among you must be your slave."

MT 20:26–27

Remember the words of the Lord Jesus, because he said, "It is more blessed to give than to receive."

AC 20:35

We also rejoice in our afflictions, because we know that affliction produces endurance, endurance produces proven character, and proven character produces hope.

RM 5:3–4

Instead, God has chosen what is foolish in the world to shame the wise, and God has chosen what is weak in the world to shame the strong.

1CO 1:27

Though he was rich, for your sake he became poor, so that by his poverty you might become rich.

2CO 8:9

Instead he emptied himself by assuming the form of a servant...for this reason God highly exalted him.

PHP 2:7–9

12 Encouragement and Prayer

Philippians 4:10–23

APPRECIATION OF SUPPORT

[10] I rejoiced in the Lord greatly because once again you renewed your care for me. You were, in fact, concerned about me but lacked the opportunity to show it. [11] I don't say this out of need, for I have learned to be content in whatever circumstances I find myself. [12] I know both how to make do with little, and I know how to make do with a lot. In any and all circumstances I have learned the secret of being content—whether well fed or hungry, whether in abundance or in need. [13] I am able to do all things through him who strengthens me. [14] Still, you did well by partnering with me in my hardship.

[15] And you Philippians know that in the early days of the gospel, when I left Macedonia, no church shared with me in the matter of giving and receiving except you alone. [16] For even in Thessalonica you sent gifts for my need several times. [17] Not that I seek the gift,

CONNECTING ACTS
TO PHILIPPIANS

Philippians 4:16

After Paul and his companions left Philippi, they headed to Thessalonica (Ac 17:1). Although the book of Acts does not tell us how Paul was supported during his time there, this note of thanks gives credit to the generous Christians of Philippi.

but I seek the profit that is increasing to your account. [18] But I have received everything in full, and I have an abundance. I am fully supplied, having received from Epaphroditus what you provided—a fragrant offering, an acceptable sacrifice, pleasing to God. [19] And my God will supply all your needs according to his riches in glory in Christ Jesus. [20] Now to our God and Father be glory forever and ever. Amen.

FINAL GREETINGS

[21] Greet every saint in Christ Jesus. The brothers who are with me send you greetings. [22] All the saints send you greetings, especially those who belong to Caesar's household. [23] The grace of the Lord Jesus Christ be with your spirit.

Proverbs 11:24–25

[24] One person gives freely,
yet gains more;
another withholds what is right,
only to become poor.

[25] A generous person will be enriched,
and the one who gives a drink of water
will receive water.

Acts 20:32–35

[32] And now I commit you to God and to the word of his grace, which is able to build you up and to give you an inheritance among all who are sanctified. [33] I have not coveted anyone's silver or gold or clothing. [34] You yourselves know that I worked with my own hands to support myself and those who are with me. [35] In every way I've shown you that it is necessary to help the weak by laboring like this and to remember the words of the Lord Jesus, because he said,

"It is more blessed to give than to receive."

2 Corinthians 9:6–9

[6] The point is this: The person who sows sparingly will also reap sparingly, and the person who sows generously will also reap generously. [7] Each person should do as he has decided in his heart—not reluctantly or out of compulsion, since God loves a cheerful giver. [8] And God is able to make every grace overflow to you, so that in every way, always having everything you need, you may excel in every good work. [9] As it is written:

He distributed freely;
he gave to the poor;
his righteousness endures forever.

1 What did you notice about this passage?

2 What questions do you have?

3 How will you respond?

Paul said he "learned" contentment (v. 11). How can you practice contentment in your current circumstances?

13 GRACE DAY

"As the Father has loved
me, I have also loved you.
Remain in my love."

JOHN 15:9

WEEK 1

WEEK 2

14 WEEKLY TRUTH

Scripture is God-breathed and true. When
we memorize it, we carry the gospel with us
wherever we go.

This week we will memorize this verse from Philippians 4, which
reminds us to dwell on things that reflect the goodness of God.

Find the corresponding memory card in the back of this book.

○ WEEK 1

● WEEK 2

Finally brothers and sisters, whatever is true, whatever is honorable, whatever is just, whatever is pure, whatever is lovely, whatever is commendable—if there is any moral excellence and if there is anything praiseworthy—dwell on these things.

PHILIPPIANS 4:8

"The secret is Christ in me, not me

in a different set of circumstances."

ELISABETH ELLIOT, *KEEP A QUIET HEART*

DOWNLOAD THE APP

VISIT
shereadstruth.com

SHOP
shopshereadstruth.com

CONTACT
hello@shereadstruth.com

CONNECT
@shereadstruth
#shereadstruth

LISTEN
She Reads Truth Podcast

Never miss a day in the Word!

Reading the Bible every day can feel like a challenge, but She Reads Truth is here to help. For just $20 a month, you can get Truth delivered right to your doorstep, so you can be a woman in the Word of God every day.

SHE READS TRUTH SUBSCRIPTION BOX BENEFITS

 Each new, beautifully designed Study Book delivered right to your door—at least one per month

 Free access to all 75+ plans on the She Reads Truth app

 Exclusive subscription swag throughout the year

 Early access to community sales

 Flexible delivery options for your monthly shipment

SHOPSHEREADSTRUTH.COM/BOX

WHERE DID I STUDY?

O HOME

O OFFICE

O COFFEE SHOP

O CHURCH

O A FRIEND'S HOUSE

O OTHER

WHAT WAS I LISTENING TO?

ARTIST:

SONG:

PLAYLIST:

WHEN DID I STUDY?

MORNING

AFTERNOON

NIGHT

What did I learn?

WHAT WAS HAPPENING IN MY LIFE?

WHAT WAS HAPPENING IN THE WORLD?

MONTH	DAY	YEAR

END DATE